AF572059

LOST IN FINANCIAL AMERICA

LOST IN FINANCIAL AMERICA

By Sy Gitelson
Illustrated by Robbie Short

LONGSTREET PRESS
Atlanta, Georgia

Published by LONGSTREET PRESS, INC.,
a subsidiary of Cox Newspapers,
a division of Cox Enterprises, Inc.
2140 Newmarket Parkway — Suite 118
Marietta, Georgia 30067

Copyright © 1993 by Sy Gitelson
Illustrations copyright © 1993 by Robbie Short

All rights reserved. No part of this book may be reproduced in any form by any means without the prior written permission of the Publisher, excepting brief quotations used in connection with reviews, written specifically for inclusion in a magazine or newspaper.

Printed in the United States of America

1st printing, 1993

ISBN: 1-56352-084-2

This book was printed by R.R. Donnelley & Sons, Harrisonburg, VA

Lost in Financial America does not offer tax, legal or investment advice. While information is based on current laws & definitions, any interpretations offered by the author are opinion.

To Shirley, Will, Hal, Ben & Don

LOST IN FINANCIAL AMERICA is the first step in understanding the confusing world of money and financial terminology — information that affects the living and buying decisions we face everyday. It's the perfect way to decipher the technical hieroglyphics and raise your financial I.Q. — in just minutes and without embarrassment. From the basic to the complex, this guide leads you through the maze of financial planning options and helps you find the one that's best for you.

LOST IN FINANCIAL AMERICA is a timely and invaluable resource that is completely reader friendly. For easy and quick reference, the book is divided into the following three alphabetically arranged parts:

MEET 'LITTLE ALERT':

Your indispensable, new "best friend" (and personal "moneymeister") who pops up throughout this book! When there's a special point to make or pitfall to avoid . . . Little Alert to the rescue!

Savings & Investment Plans

- Annuities
- Asset Management Accounts
- Bonds
- Cafeteria Plans
- Certificates of Deposit ("CD")
- Collectibles
- 401(K)s
- GICs
- Ginnie Maes (Government National Mortgage Association)
- Home Equity Loans
- Interest Paying Checking
- IRAs
- KEOGHS (commonly called HR-10s)
- Limited Partnerships
- Money Market Accounts
- Mutual Funds
- Passbook Savings Accounts
- Penny Stocks
- Pension Plans
- Real Estate Investment Trusts (REITs)
- Reverse Mortgages
- SEPs (Simplified Employee Plans)
- Social Security
- SPDAs ("Spiders")
- Stocks
- Treasury Bills,
  Notes & Bonds

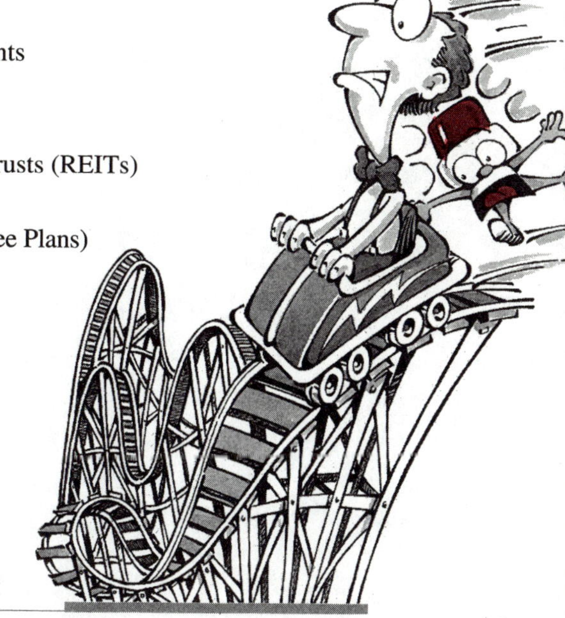

Annuities are a kind of long-term, tax-deferred Certificate of Deposit, offered by an insurance company. Try to visualize an annuity in two phases: (1) the time you pay into the plan, and (2) the time you start receiving benefits. There are options and choices for both phases.

The "Pay-In" or Savings Phase: Put simply, you can put money in the plan in one lump sum (called a **single premium**), or periodically through a series of contributions (called a **flexible annuity**). Generally, you are offered a guaranteed interest rate (somewhat higher than a conventional savings plan). Another type, called the **variable annuity**, gives you the option of having your money invested in growth-based investments instead of the CD-type interest account. In fact, various insurance companies have gone into partnership with some of the country's best known mutual funds. Others have created their own stock or bond accounts. Regardless of where you put your money, *all earnings are tax deferred until you receive them*.

The "Pay-Out" or Benefit Phase: Benefits usually begin at retirement (or some future time) and can be received in a variety of ways. You can take all your money out in one lump sum or elect an income-type plan. The size of your income payment is based on how much money is in your plan — and for how long you want to receive benefits. A lifetime pay-out guarantees a set income for as long as you live. It ends with you. *(However,* *most plans will allow you to take a reduced benefit so payments can be continued to your spouse upon your death.)* Others last for only a specific period of time (giving you a bigger benefit.) In most cases, your benefits are *not fully taxable* since a portion of the money you receive is a return of your own principal (or initial investment).

KEEP IN MIND! Annuities have "loads" or built-in sales commissions and fees. Yet, for many well-off people who have a long-term savings horizon, annuities can provide very attractive tax-deferred returns — although the variable annuity has some investment risk. **(See Mutual Fund/Stock Sections.)** Morningstar, Inc. (800-876-5005) provides "performance reports" for most of the major plans, as does Annuity & Life Insurance Shopper (800-872-6684) for the fixed-rate plans.

Alert! ***With most annuities, your money is tied up for a long period of time and is only as safe as the insurance company behind it! Should you need to withdraw funds, you could get hit with a "surrender" charge. Plus, your earnings will be subject to federal income tax*** **and** ***a 10% federal penalty if you touch that money before age 59 1/2. (You can, however, "roll it over" to another company.) Don't fall for various*** **"Bonus Interest"** ***come-ons, which you get to keep only if you choose a long pay-out period way down the road. Finally, watch out for "loss leader" interest rates that drop after the first year!***

Asset Management Accounts give you the ability to combine a variety of financial services in a single account. Offered by most large brokerage houses (and many banks), they allow you to buy and sell securities; to open a free ("no check limit") checking account or a money market fund for your cash balance and other earnings; to use a credit card; even to enjoy the automatic payment of bills (like your mortgage) etc. — and receive one, consolidated monthly statement. If you have a lot of financial transactions going on, these accounts can make your life easier. (The interest earned on any cash balances usually offsets the service charge.) Asset Management Accounts don't manage anything, they simply follow your instructions.

Bonds are simply IOUs between you and the issuer, which is generally a corporation or government agency. While a stockholder is an "owner," a bond holder is a creditor . Bonds are considered "debt instruments" because the issuer owes you and promises to repay you plus interest at some future date. (Bonds can be bought at full face value or — like a U.S. Savings bond — "discounted" by the amount of interest that's ultimately earned.) If you buy a bond when it's first issued, you can't lose money if you hold it to maturity — unless the issuer defaults (or goes bankrupt). Should that occur, bond holders get paid off before any stockholders.

The Major types of Bonds are:

- U.S. Savings Bonds
- Government (Treasury Bills, Notes & Bonds)
- Municipals (Tax Free)
- Corporate

Bonds — not held to maturity —trade up and down just like stocks. Unlike newly issued bonds (which sell at "par" or face value), already issued — or "used bonds" — trade in their own secondary market. *With stock, earnings are the key to success. With bonds it's the interest rate — and how well that rate stacks up against rates available elsewhere!* Suppose you have a bond that pays 8% interest while the "going rate" (at the bank and elsewhere) is 5%. Should you want to sell that bond, many investors will pay extra — *or a premium* — to get it. (Your $1,000 face amount bond may bring you $1,200.) On the other hand, if interest rates were to climb to 10% or so, your 8% bond is no longer in demand and could sell at a loss — or at discount. Again, bonds trade actively just like any other security — with some investors willing to pay extra to get the higher interest rate while others are more than willing to sell for a profit.

KEEP IN MIND! You can also see why bonds, particularly long-term ones, can be susceptible to market risk every time there's even a threat of a rise in interest rates. **The Rule of Thumb:** *Bond prices go in the opposite direction of interest rates!*

Another key to bond prices is inflation. If investors feel inflation is not a real threat, the steady income of bonds adds to their appeal. *Again, if you buy a bond at issue and hold it to maturity, none of this matters.* By the way, some corporate bonds are convertible, which means they can be exchanged for the corporation's common stock (if you like the company's growth prospects.) You'll have to give up about 1% in yield to get this feature.

Alert! ***Find out if the bond is "callable," which means the issuer can "call in" or redeem the bond before its maturity date. For example, municipality X has a bunch of outstanding bonds paying 10% interest. They decide to refinance that "debt" to take advantage of the recent drop in interest rates. So municipality X issues new bonds at 6% using that money to pay off those older bond holders — and gain a savings of 4% in interest payments! This could cost you if you just paid extra to get that 10% bond and it gets "called"— not to mention the loss of that high interest income you were getting!***

KEEP IN MIND! There is a difference between "rate" and "yield." Yield takes into account the current value of the bond as well as its interest rate. For example, a bond paying 8% isn't yielding 8% if you paid a premium for it (or more than face amount)!

Bonds are only as safe as the issuer behind them. They range from highly speculative ("junk," which pay above-average returns), to those federally guaranteed (like savings bonds) *As with most investments, the higher the return potential, the higher the risk.* Standard & Poor's and Moody's rate the quality of bonds from the highest (AAA and Aaa respectively) to those in default (D and C respectively).

Bonds pay interest generally two ways: (1) You receive a check directly from the issuer quarterly or semiannually, etc., as spelled out at the time of purchase. (This used to be done by clipping "coupons" attached to the bond and sending them in for payment). **(2)** You receive your interest all at once when the bond matures. **These are called "Zeros."** With Zeros, the issuer "discounts" the bond *below* its face value, paying you full face amount later on when you redeem them. A good example is a Series EE U.S. Savings bond where you pay half the face value today and collect the full face value later. For instance, you pay $500 for a $1,000 bond. The difference between what you pay for the bond and the bond's higher face amount at maturity is the interest accrued — or in our previous example, $500. (The EEs presently issued are guaranteed to double in 18 years even though you can keep earning interest up to 30 years after issue — called "extended maturities.") Unless the bond is a tax-free municipal or Series EE savings bond, you still pay taxes on the interest that's credited each year (called "imputed") *even though you don't receive it.* "STRIPS" are essentially U.S. Treasury Zeros. They too separate the income and principal components of the bond. **See section "Treasury Bills, Notes & Bonds."**

Alert! ***Hold Zeros until they mature because interest accrues at a faster pace toward the end.***

Tax-Free Municipal Bonds Versus Taxable-Yield

When does it make sense to sacrifice a higher return for tax-free income? It all depends on your tax bracket, which determines the after-tax dollars you'll keep. Here's a fast way to figure out whether it's worthwhile for you : (1) Subtract your "tax bracket % rate" from the number 1.00. (For example, if you're in the 28% bracket, it would be

1.00 minus .28 = .72.) (2) Divide that number into the tax free "muni" interest rate to find the equivalent taxable return. (Let's assume you're considering a 6% tax-free bond. If you divide that 6% by the .72 calculated above, you'll need a taxable return of 8.3% to do as well as the "muni.") If you're in the 15% bracket, you probably shouldn't consider "tax-frees" at all. The numbers just don't add up!

KEEP IN MIND! Special Educational Savings Bond Program through the purchase of Series EE Savings Bonds. Series EE Savings Bonds permit you two options in reporting interest on your tax return: **(1)** on a yearly basis as you earn it, or (2) postpone all tax due until maturity. If you select option #2, meet the IRS's income limitation, and use the money for a child's college education, you pay no income tax on the interest accumulated. You can buy up to $15,000 of these bonds ($30,000 face amount) each year. Remember, these are discounted savings bonds, unlike series HH U.S. Savings Bonds, which are "current income" securities. (That means EEs pay all interest at maturity while HHs send you a check every 6 months over their 10-year maturity term.)

Cafeteria Plans are flexible employee benefit plans where the individual gets to choose (within limits) his/her own benefits. Company dollars earmarked for benefits are combined with employee contributions to provide a kind of “flexible spending account.” There are valuable tax breaks involved as well.

Certificate of Deposit (CD) is a promissory note between you and the savings institution. Most — but not all — are backed by the Federal Government (FDIC). The bank (or S&L) promises to return your principal plus all interest when the period you select is up. They are called “time deposit” accounts because your money is locked in for the length of the commitment (as opposed to “on-demand” savings/checking accounts where there is no wait).

Alert! ***Consider how fast you think saving rates may rise in the future. Pick shorter maturities or even a money market account if you think they're on their way up. Be wary of “CD Alternatives” — any of a number of plans not FDIC insured! Many are simply marketing ploys to get CD money from consumers frustrated over falling interest rates.***

Collectibles, such as coins, antiques, even baseball cards, etc., have potential for increasing in value, particularly those that have not yet benefited from an organized collectors' market. Most people who get involved with collectibles do so for enjoyment as well as profit.

4 **01(K)s** are company-sponsored benefit plans that allow employees to put part of their paycheck into a tax-deferred savings/investment program. They are called "salary reduction" plans since they "reduce" your salary by the amount you put in the plan — thus lowering your taxable pay! (For example, if you make $30,000 a year and invest $3,000, only $27,000 appears on your W-2 form.) In many cases, employers match, in some part, the employees' contributions. Plans vary in terms of savings options, with many offering fixed interest to mutual-fund growth-based choices. You have to act as your own money manager picking the plan (or combination of plans) that's right for you. **See Mutual Fund Section.** *Plus, you can "income average" your retirement benefits — unlike an IRA which taxes you on the amount withdrawn.* There is probably no other employee benefit — in terms of tax advantages, employer "matching funds" and individual choice — so valuable! (There is, however, a 10% penalty for withdrawing funds before age 59½.) For charitable and educational organizations, these plans are called 403(b). You'll pay some management and overhead fees which should not total more than 1% a year. **(See Pension Plan section.)**

G **ICs** are a "fixed interest" savings option available in many, if not all, pension plans. They offer you a safe place to put your retirement dollars if you don't want to invest in more risky stock and bond accounts.

Alert! ***While these "Guaranteed Investment Contracts" have been promoted as a rock-solid "CD"-type account, some have been on shaky ground. Your money is only as safe as the insurance company backing the account. There is no federal agency protection.***

Ginnie Maes (Government National Mortgage Association) are essentially "pools" of home mortgages packaged and sold to the general public as a security. They are backed by the federal government and trade just like any other security. As homeowners make their mortgage payments each month, the money passes through the Ginnie Mae to each investor as their share of those payments. You can buy Ginnie Maes through a broker ($25,000 minimum) or through a mutual fund that specializes in them. Although not completely risk free, they combine safety and historically high yields — out-performing long term Triple A Rated Bonds and 10-year Treasury Notes on the average.

Alert! ***Your total monthly payment includes principal as well as interest. So when all the mortgages are eventually paid off, your Ginnie Maes have no value. (Your "initial investment" has been completely returned.) Ginnie Maes, like bonds, are affected by swings in interest rates. For example, when rates drop, homeowners tend to pay off their mortgages more quickly. When that happens, you get your money back sooner and that high yield comes to an end! On the average, Ginnie Maes last about eight years.***

Home Equity Loans allow you to borrow the equity out of your home at an interest rate lower than most personal loans. These "second mortgage" loans have become very popular because the *interest on up to $100,000 borrowed is tax deductible* with little or no out-of-pocket closing costs. You can get the money through (1) a line of credit which you can draw upon like one big credit card, or (2) a single cash sum (called a "closed-end" loan) usually repayable in monthly installments. Many banks offer variable as well as fixed-interest loans (just like a first mortgage).

Alert! ***These loans use your house as collateral. Fail to make payments, and you could face repossession. Remember you are spending your equity — with most people using the money to consolidate and pay off their debts. You may want to check out a variable loan with a convertible option. This lets you switch over to a fixed-interest loan if rates start to go up!***

Interest Paying Checking — commonly called "NOW" accounts — credit simple interest on your checking account balance. In most cases, they have minimum balance requirements and fees.

IRAs are Individual Retirement Accounts — kind of your own private pension plan where *both your contributions and earnings are not taxable until you take the money out.* IRAs were principally created for those individuals not covered under company pension plans. Currently, you can write off up to $2,000 ($2,250 if you include a non-working spouse); $4,000 if you and your spouse both work. However — even if you are in a company pension plan — you can still *fully* participate if you make under $25,000 individually (or $40,000 if married filing jointly). You can participate on a partial tax-deductible basis if you make less than $35,000 individually — $50,000 for married couples. Your money can be invested with a bank or mutual fund, which will easily set up and administer your account. *(The IRA is simply the framework for any of a variety of plans you choose over the years.)* You can take all or part of your money out as early as age 59½ without penalty. You must start taking funds out by age 70½. It's a plan every eligible person should take advantage of even if you can't put the entire $2,000 away each year. (Only the amount you invest can be deducted.) You can even wait until April 15 of the following year to make your contribution. (For example, 1993 contributions can be made anytime up to April 15, 1994.) Some accounts handled by brokerage companies are called **"Self-Directed" IRAs** because you have a choice (and convenience) of stocks, CDs, Treasuries, mutual funds, etc., within one "custodian" account. You can move between investments easily and quickly and get one overall statement at year end.

Alert! ***While a "Self-Directed" IRA has its advantages, the fees (both maintenance and transaction) can leave your account a little lighter.***

KEOGHS — commonly called **HR-10s** — are retirement plans for the self-employed (who are not incorporated). For the most part, they permit up to 15% (a maximum of $30,000 each year) to be deducted from your gross earnings. You must put the same percentage away for each covered employee if you have any. (And depending on the type of KEOGH, you may be locked into making annual contributions.) They are, in a sense, a super IRA since you can invest much higher amounts than the $2,000 yearly limit. They have approximately the same withdrawal restrictions. *However, you do get the tax advantage of forward averaging when you take a lump sum retirement settlement.* **See Separate Rollover — Forward Averaging Section.**

Limited Partnerships (RELPs) are groups of investors who "pool their resources" to buy a variety of income-producing real estate properties or (to a much lesser extent) heavy equipment, livestock, oil & gas drilling, etc. Before 1986, limited partnerships were bought almost exclusively as tax shelters with the deductions — in many cases — worth more than the actual dollar amount invested. Today, people who invest in RELPs do so primarily for income. (The General Partner really calls the shots and often gets the lion's share of the rewards, if any.)

Alert! ***Limited partnerships are not for the timid investor and require patience and commitment because once you're in, you're stuck until all the properties are sold. (A Real Estate Investment Trust, called* REIT, *is different.* See separate section.*) Moreover, many people have really taken a bath — falling victim to inflated returns that include part of your original investment.***

Money Market Account — is a savings account that pays you a higher interest rate when your balance reaches (and maintains) a certain level. The rate credited to your account usually changes weekly. You have no withdrawal restrictions and are allowed to write a limited number of checks.

Mutual Funds are a kind of "investment cooperative" where your money and that of thousands of others are pooled together (under the direction of a professional fund manager) to buy a selection of stocks, bonds or other securities. Key advantages of mutual funds are (1) the small investor with limited knowledge and resources can participate for as little as $200, getting the same cost, service and current intelligence as the large investor; (2) *diversification* — since most funds invest in 50 to 200 different securities at any one time, reducing the risk of investing in only one single company; (3) they are customer friendly, offering ease in buying and selling shares, toll-free account access, simplified statements, etc.

A Mutual Fund Share represents your piece of the fund's various holdings. Each share is priced daily by adding up the value of all its investments, subtracting any expenses and debts, and dividing the balance by the number of outstanding shares. This is called the "net asset value" — the price per share that appears daily in your newspaper. Mutual funds create profit two ways: from dividends (or interest) earned by any of the individual securities in the fund *or* when the fund manager sells any of those securities for more than he paid for them — called a capital gain. (Managers generally buy and sell holdings all the time to attempt to maximize returns within the fund's objectives.) Funds continually issue new shares to new investors and buy them back at any time. Remember, funds can be "groups" or a "mixture" of many things, not just stocks.

"Mattress Stuffers" to "High Rollers"

There are some 3,800 mutual funds and they generally fall into 3 broad categories — stock, bond and balanced (kind of a combination of the first 2). They range from the extremely safe to the highly volatile — or from Money Market to Ultra Growth. While the Money Market invests only in rock-solid, fixed-interest plans —your principal is not in jeopardy and the $1 share price never changes — the pay-off is limited. On the other hand, the ultra-aggressive funds offer the best opportunity for hitting the jackpot (since they go after the smaller, yet-to-be discovered companies), but investors must have the financial and emotional staying power to ride out the down times. For the younger investor, investment risk is somewhat neutralized over a period of years. *You have to make the trade-off: How much risk can you handle in reaching for the brass ring?*

Within the major categories, mutual funds come in all variations, including :

- **Aggressive Growth/Growth** — tries to pick tomorrow's big winners today by investing in highly promising but less established stocks.
- **Income** — emphasizes high yields from bonds, preferred or high-dividend-paying stocks.
- **Balanced** — spreads out investments between stocks, bonds and other securities to cover all the bases.
- **Money Market** — seeks income while protecting principle by investing in very short-term, virtually "risk-free" obligations. There are 3 types — General, Government Only and Tax Free.
- **Bond** — provides income through government or corporate bonds of similar maturities.

• **Municipal Bond** — offers tax-free income by investing in tax-exempt municipal bonds. Some are insured by private companies, not the U.S. Government.

• **Sector** — limits investments to specific industries like health care, financial services, etc.

• **International /Global** — targets foreign stocks or bonds with some specializing in specific regions like Europe or The Pacific.

• **Index** — sort of a "copy-cat" fund which picks an established, closely watched index like the **S&P 500** and invests only in those companies.

KEEP IN MIND! Virtually all the major mutual fund companies have a family of different funds — so you can split your investments — even swap funds through a phone call with little or no charge. In a "Bull" market (where stocks rise broadly and continually), aggressive growth funds have done the best and conservative funds the worst; in a "Bear" market (where stocks fall broadly and continually), aggressive growth funds have dipped the most while the conservative ones have suffered the least. The same forces that cause individual stocks and bonds to rise and fall also come into play.

See separate sections.

Alert! ***Watch out for "load" funds where you pay a sales charge (or broker commission) as high as 8.5% up front, or up to 1.5% when you sell (like a redemption fee). Even though many of these funds have done quite well, it's still a big pill to swallow. Also ask if the fund has a "12b-l charge" — a "pass-on" marketing and operating expense;*** **check the 5-year expense projection in the prospectus —** ***it's usually on page 2; get the history of the fund's performance over time (not just an isolated year) — Morningstar and Lipper are just two rating services that can help. Consider the Fund Manager's track record for at least five years as well.***

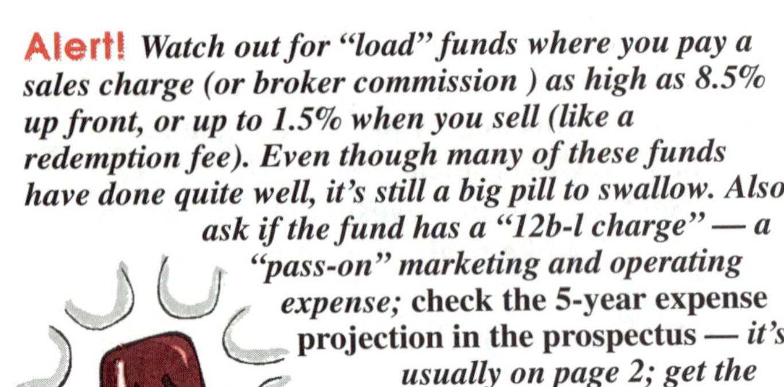

KEEP IN MIND! There is a difference between open-end (the most common type) and closed-end mutual funds. *Closed-end don't issue new shares.* They sell a set number to the public — then close the door. Shares trade up or down (like one big stock or bond) on the major exchanges. They can sell at premium or discount depending on how in-favor, or out-of-favor, the fund becomes.

Mutual Fund Taxation is similar to stock. **(See Stock section.)** Keep in mind the securities in each fund *individually* generate dividends (or interest).

At year end you will receive a 1099 indicating the total amount of these earnings distributed to you in cash or in additional shares. When you sell your fund, you'll also incur a "capital gain" if you sell your shares for more than you paid for them (and vice versa in terms of a "capital loss"). To report a gain or loss on your tax return, you must cash in, or sell, your shares. Until then, you have incurred only a "paper" loss or gain.

Passbook Savings Account — pays you a stated interest rate with no withdrawal restrictions. You're notified anytime there is a rate change.

Penny Stocks are cheap stocks usually defined as those selling under $5 per share. There has been a lot of fraud in the marketing of these very high-risk, untested securities with many unsuspecting (and gullible) people getting suckered.

Pension Plans structure retirement benefits in two general ways: **(1) Defined Benefit Plans** — where you know how much you'll get (and for how long) but not how much it will cost your company to foot the bill; and **(2) Defined-Contribution Plans** — where the company's contribution level stays the same, but how much you'll eventually get is determined at retirement. *(No matter how the plan is structured, the way these pension funds are prudently managed have an overwhelming effect on both company profits and the safety of your future benefits. Moreover, the* *government agency that protects private pension plans — the Pension Benefit Guaranty Corp. — is in tough financial shape due to the underfunding of many company plans.)* Under a typical pension plan, benefits are computed on years of service and your salary level over the last 5 years or so of employment. Generally, these are your peak earning years. You'll probably receive in the neighborhood of 30% of pay unless you retire early — before age 65. If you do retire early, you normally get two choices: (1) reduced benefits that start almost immediately; (2) the option to delay full benefits until you reach age 65.

Here's a quick definition of some popular types of "qualified" (or government approved) plans:

- **Thrift Plan** lets you contribute part of your income in investments like a mutual fund or annuity with your employer providing matching funds up to a specific limit.
- **Employee Stock Ownership Plans** (or ESOPs) give you stock in the company you work for. (It's non-voting stock.) ESOPs alone — without any other retirement plan — can be risky because the value of your benefits rise and fall exclusively with your own company stock.
- **Profit Sharing Plan** permits a company to contribute a portion of company profits for employees without committing to a fixed percentage schedule every year. In fact, contributions can be skipped even in profitable years.

• **Money Purchase Plan** allows a company to set up a contribution schedule based on a percentage of your income and not company profits. (Up to 25% of personal salary is possible.)

• **Deferred-Compensation Plans** are essentially "salary reduction" plans. That means, your contributions can be subtracted from your earnings (dropping your adjusted gross income). For example, if you make $30,000 a year and set aside $3,000 a year, your actual salary for income tax purposes is $27,000. **(See 401 K section.)** Employers often match your contributions at some level.

Alert! ***You should keep track of your pension plan not only in terms of retirement income but also the amount of benefits you own (called "vested") that are yours if you change jobs or stop working altogether. You have a legal right to get this information from your company every year. If you are offered early retirement, you have to check out the math. Are you willing to trade a reduction in benefits for the chance to get your pension before age 65!*** **(Also see ERISA section.)**

Real Estate Investment Trusts (REITs) are essentially "mutual funds" of real estate properties and are traded like stocks on any of the major exchanges. They can possess good income-producing potential since they are required to pay out 95% of their earnings each year to investors. Importantly, the income generated can be tax sheltered in whole or part due to mortgage interest deductions and depreciation of the properties. Unlike a Limited Partnership **(see separate section)**, REITs are "liquid" and are easily bought and sold. *There is a downside: Earnings fluctuate with a notoriously volatile real estate market.*

Reverse Mortgages allow homeowners (generally senior citizens age 62 and older), who have little or no mortgage left, the ability to draw equity out of their home in monthly income payments. By tapping into the equity in their house while still alive, owners supplement their retirement income on a tax-free basis since payments are considered loans. While very appropriate for many, the loan is repaid from your estate, leaving less for your heirs.

Alert! ***It is possible to outlive your income payments (by draining out all your equity), which could leave you out on the street — literally!***

SEPs — Simplified Employee Plans — are extremely easy-to-set-up pension plans designed for all types of small (or one-person) businesses. Also called "super IRAs," annual contribution limits are similar to a KEOGH — both permit 15% of your income up to $30,000 max. But unlike the KEOGH, *there is no annual IRS form to be filed* and yearly contributions can be skipped. (Some KEOGHs don't have that contribution flexibility.) SEPs do have a drawback at retirement time: lump-sum benefits can*not* be "forward averaged." **(See Rollover — Forward Averaging Section.)** Contributions made for employees (which must be at the same percentage level as the owner) are also considered a fully tax-deductible business expense.

Social Security benefit estimates can be found by calling **800-234-5772.** It's all computerized and your level of benefits can be easily determined. You can apply up to 3 months before you want benefits to begin and *you will need all or some of the following:* your social security number; your birth certificate; your W-2 forms or self-employment tax return for last year; your discharge form if you served in the Armed Forces; your spouse's birth certificate and social security number if he or she is applying for benefits; children's birth certificates and social security numbers, if applying for children's benefits; and your checking or savings account information, if you want direct deposit.

Alert! ***If you plan on working after Social Security benefits begin, payments will be decreased if you earn more than a certain amount. Starting in 1993, people 65 — 69 lose $1 of benefits for every $3 they earn above $10,560. Recipients under age 65 (who receive reduced benefits because they chose to begin benefits early) lose $1 for every $2 they earn over $7,680 a year. When you reach age 70, you can earn all you want. Many people approaching retirement are faced with the following choice: "Do I start drawing reduced benefits (at 80% of maximum) early at age 62 or wait until age 65 and collect full benefits?" Statistically, the age-65 retiree generally won't catch up with the 3-year "head start" of the 62-year-old retiree (who invests those benefits).***

The threshold to determine if part of your social security benefits are taxable is $32,000 *in adjusted gross income* for married couples filing jointly. It's $25,000 for single filers, qualifying widows or widowers and zero for married people (who live together) filing separate returns. If you exceed those amounts, 50% of your benefits are taxed — *85% if current proposals become law.*

KEEP IN MIND! For all you wage earners, FICA — which are Social Security and Medicare taxes — are on the rise again. You'll pay a total of 7.65% on the first $57,600 of salary in 1993 before the major portion of the tax stops. The Medicare portion — 1.45% — continues until your pay reaches $135,000.

Unlike Medicare, the Social Security system is currently in pretty good shape, running at a healthy surplus. What happens in the years ahead (when all the "baby boomers" qualify) is another story.

SPDA (Standard & Poor's Depository Receipt) is a unit investment trust that essentially invests in all the stocks tracked by the S&P. Commonly referred to as "spiders," SPDAs let you *capture the market* through one purchase. While they trade like a single stock, they offer broad diversification (since you're getting a piece of all 500 companies) and relatively low expense charges. Dividends are paid quarterly. Expect "spiders" to rise and fall in value with the performance of the S&P. (Call 1-800-THE AMEX for more info.)

Stocks represent ownership (or "equity') in a publicly held company. Essentially, there are two types of stock: (1) common, which pays (or doesn't pay) dividends based on how well the company performed in the current year, or (2) preferred, which pays fixed dividends no matter how the company does. Should a company go bankrupt, preferred shareholders get paid off before common shareholders.

Stocks Can Make You Money in Two Ways **(1)** through cash **dividend**s paid directly to you as your portion of company's earnings (or much less often, as additional shares), and **(2)** if you sell the stock for more than you paid for it. That profit is called a **capital gain.** Conversely, sell it for less, and you suffer a **capital loss.** (Do it after a year, and it's called long term.) Companies generally pay dividends quarterly — called "record" dates. You have to own the stock at least 4 business days before the record date to get the dividend — or the previous owner gets it. If you buy the stock during the 4-day period, however, the price you pay is reduced by the amount of the lost dividend. (When this happens — the stock goes "ex-dividend." That's what the little "x" means besides the stock quotation in the newspaper.) *If stocks could be transferred between buyer and seller on the same day they are traded, there would be no need for this "ex-dividend" period. It's simply an equitable way to handle a dividend when it's distributed close to the record date.*

Stocks Range from the *Steady-As-You-Go* to *the High Flyers!* For example, the "white knuckle" investor looking for steady **dividend** income — almost like a bond — might find utility stocks just the ticket. Other investors chase the "big carrot" of **capital growth** (the future rise in share price) found in many new, emerging companies. **(See IPO & Stock Exchange sections.)**

Stock Splits generally create more shares at a lower price. Suppose you own 100 shares of Company X stock trading at $20 each before the company declares a 2-for-1 split. After the split you'll own 200 shares (instead of the 100 you had) but their value will be halved to $10. You have not gained or lost a penny since your investment is still worth $2,000. Companies do it to make their stock more affordable to new, small investors. Many also believe — and lots of times it happens — the stock will climb more quickly at the new lower price. (A **Reverse Split** does just the opposite — fewer shares are created at a higher price.)

Alert! ***Although historically the most rewarding in terms of overall return, the stock market suffers from unpredictable, erratic mood swings. It's even manipulated by the large corporate/pension managers with their computer driven "buy & sell" programs. Avoid "can't miss" tips, get-rich-quick advice, your own gut reaction to new fads. The golden rule: Buy good stocks; watch them closely; stick with them patiently for the long term. When reaching for the brass ring, be prepared to accept risk financially and temperamentally. Have a plan and start investing only when you've set aside an emergency nest egg.***

KEEP IN MIND! The economy — and stock market — usually prosper in periods of low interest rates, low inflation and sustained business growth. It falters when the opposite occurs. Companies with low debt, strong market share and a solid performance record are always good prospects.

- **Calculating a Stock's Yield** is done by dividing the annual dividends paid per share by the share's trading price. For example, if ABC Widget Company paid $1.20 in total dividends during the year and the stock is selling at $20, its yield is 6% — or $1.20 divided by $20. (An effective yield is slightly higher because it factors in the compounding effect of reinvesting earnings.)

- **Calculating Total Return** includes changes in the stock's value plus its yield. Let's assume the per-share price of ABC (see previous example) grew from $18 to $20 during the year. The $2 increase divided by the $18 original share price equals an 11% return. Add that 11% increase in stock value to the 6% yield and the total return is 17%.

Treasury Bills, Notes & Bonds are all "debt" securities — or super safe IOUs between you and the United States Treasury. They are distinguished by the length of their maturities: T-Bills can be purchased for a period of 13, 26 or 52 weeks. (There is a $10,000 minimum.) Notes can be bought in 1- to 5-year maturities in $1,000 to $5,000 denominations; bonds are available in medium (5- to 10-year) and long-term (10- to 40-year) maturities. *The longer the term of the bond, the higher the interest rate.* Notes and bonds pay interest semiannually, while bills are bought at discount, which means you get all your interest at maturity. "STRIPS" are like Treasury "Zeros" (issued and sold way below their face value.) **See Bond Section**. You can buy any of these IOUs through a bank, stock broker or by yourself through a "treasury direct" account at the Federal Reserve Bank— and pay *no* sales commission. Under Treasury Direct, you'll get an ongoing statement from the government (no certificate is issued) with all interest electronically deposited in your personal bank account. None of the above is exempt from federal income taxes — *but they are from state taxes.* Every January, you'll get a form 1099-OID indicating the interest you've earned during the past year.

The Higher the Return, the Greater the Risk !
Pros and cons of principal wealth-generating plans:

	PROS	CONS
Savings accounts	Very Safe	Modest Return
Stocks	Excellent growth potential	Volatility/ risk of loss
Bonds	Secure/stable income	No growth of "principal"
............................Municipals	Tax Free Interest (Fed.)	Lower returns
Mutual Funds ...Growth	Excellent growth potential	Some risk/fewer dividends
............................Income	More stable . . . stresses dividends/interest income	Less big growth potential
Annuities ....Fixed	Tax-deferred interest	Locked in for specific term/ Withdrawal fees
............................Variable	Tax-deferred growth	Risk associated with any stock investment
Real Estate	Long-term appreciation	Periodic down turns/ Little liquidity

KEEP IN MIND! Market Risk is the chance your investment could lose part — even all — of its value.

Purchasing Power Risk is the chance your investment won't keep up with inflation. (If you're earning a safe 5%, but inflation is running at 6%, you're losing buying power.)

Pay Yourself First is one of the first rules of building wealth. Simply put, you should include personal savings and investment dollars in your budgeting and bill paying. Your first obligation is to yourself.

Insurance Plans

- Automobile insurance
- Cobra
- Credit Life (& Accident) Insurance
- Dental Insurance
- Disability Insurance
- Health Insurance
- Homeowner's/Renter's insurance
- Liability Insurance
- Life Insurance
- Long Term Nursing Home Care Insurance
- Medicaid
- Medicare
- Supplemental Medicare Insurance
- Title Insurance
- Umbrella Policies

Automobile insurance is a package of several types of coverage divided into two general groups: **(1) Bodily Injury and Property Damage Liability** — *if you hurt someone or destroy someone's property* (usually required in most states), and **(2) Physical Damage** — *if you wreck your own car* (usually not required by law). Other parts of the package can include medical payments, uninsured motorist protection, collision insurance, comprehensive (which covers just about anything that could happen to your car not covered by collision), towing, etc. The sum of these parts adds up to your total premium. You can reduce or increase your cost by changing the amounts of each part — or by eliminating certain coverages not required by law. *(For example, if you have an old jalopy not worth very much, the cost of physical damage could be almost as much as the car's value if stolen or destroyed.)*

No Fault Insurance permits a policyholder's own company to pay for injuries and lost income regardless of who is at fault in an accident. It was intended to streamline the claims system by eliminating the need to sue other drivers to gain economic compensation. The log jam occurs in areas like "pain and suffering" not covered by no-fault. It's back to court for even a relatively small dispute.

C**obra** is a federal program that extends your group health insurance for at least 18 months should you leave your job (where you were covered). You pay for this interim coverage, to which your former employer is required to give you access.

C**redit Life (& Accident) Insurance** is designed to pay off a loan if you die (or become disabled). It is a kind of term insurance that (theoretically) reduces in line with your outstanding loan balance.

Alert! ***Watch your step! As a general rule, this type of coverage is not a good value and is usually not needed. It's better to buy one single policy that covers all your exposures .***

Dental Insurance covers all routine dental work (including bridgework or dentures) as well as oral surgery. It is added as an option to many health insurance packages, with the insurer paying 80% of the charges after a separate deductible is satisfied. Cosmetic work is seldom covered.

Disability Insurance is essentially a "salary continuation" plan that insures a portion of your earned income in case of prolonged illness or accident. Policies vary according to how much they pay, for how long, how soon they start, and importantly — what they consider a disability.

Alert! ***The definition of disability is critical. Can you do any work at all? Are you unable to work at your current job? Try to get a policy that's "noncancellable," which means it can't be cancelled or the rates increased for any reason, as long as you pay your premium. "Guaranteed Renewable" is a noncancellable policy but with rates that can be raised. They can't go up individually but they can as a group for everyone who has that type (or "class") of coverage.***

Health Insurance can generally be divided in three categories, (1) **Traditional**, (2) **HMOs**, and (3) **PPOs**. Under a traditional plan, you pay the bill, file a claim and get reimbursed by your insurance company. (Sometimes, you can "assign benefits," which simply means the doctor or hospital can "bill" and receive payment directly from the insurer.) Once your deductible is met (the amount you have to pay before coverage kicks in), the insurance company typically pays 80% of covered medical expenses. The 20% you pay is called a **co-payment** which stops once you reach a certain level of out-of-pocket expense, in most cases around $2,000. (Such provisions are called "stop loss" because your financial exposure ends.) The traditional "fee for service" plan is more expensive, but you have complete freedom to choose your own doctor and hospital with immediate access for routine visits no matter where you are in the country. An **HMO** (Health Maintenance Organization) is a prepaid plan that charges only a small fee per doctor visit (no matter how frequently you seek services). There is a nominal charge for prescription drugs with *no* deductibles or claims to file. While very cost effective, particularly for families who need preventive care, you must use doctors and hospitals provided or authorized by the HMO except in emergencies. (A **POS** — Point Of Service — plan is a cousin to the HMO, where a primary care physician guides you through a specific network of approved providers.) A **PPO** — Preferred Provider Organization — combines some elements of both the traditional and HMO plans. With a PPO, you have a much larger network of doctors to choose from. You can also go to doctors outside the network, but you will pay more. The cost per visit is more than an HMO, but less than traditional coverage.

Alert! ***The decision you must make is: Do you choose a doctor in a restricted "managed network" or stick with your own doctor and pay more of the cost? Plus, with an HMO or POS network, you're at the mercy of the general (or primary care) physician who alone decides what services are needed and should be ordered. The doctor serves as a gatekeeper who can open the door to further medical help — or slam it shut. Furthermore, there have been complaints about the long waiting time for non-urgent appointments with some HMOs.***

See Managed Competition in last section.

KEEP IN MIND!

- If you have, or are considering, a traditional plan, compare the premium cost savings of selecting a higher deductible. It could be a much better buy.
- Most traditional plans only pay for what they call "usual, customary and reasonable" expenses. If your company determines your bills exceed this level, you'll have to pick up the difference on top of any co-payment or deductible, etc. Plus, many of these "free choice" plans also require second opinions, up-front approval to go to the hospital (called "precertification") and other restrictions.
- For those on or close to retirement, there's a move by companies to cut — or trim — health benefits for retirees. Due to a new accounting rule (called Financial Accounting Standard 106), the estimated future expense of these health benefits — which can run in the billions of dollars for the Fortune 500–size corporation — must now be figured into the company's current earnings. Aimed at making investors more aware of a company's ultimate obligations, the rule can make a big dent in a business's bottom line and may prompt major cutbacks in these benefits. Retirees, particularly uninsurable ones, can be left out in the cold — or forced to pick up more of the tab.

Homeowner's / Renter's insurance covers most of the catastrophes that can befall your house — fire, lightning, burglary, falling trees, etc. — as well as any liability risk from being sued.

Called "multi-peril," policies do differ in what "perils" they cover. (An HO-3 policy covers the widest variety of disasters.) You may need an even broader policy to protect against such things as bursting water pipes, flood and earthquake losses, etc. Buy a "replacement cost" policy to protect you against inflationary costs of rebuilding after a catastrophe. For items like jewelry, collectibles or electronic equipment, you'll probably need a separate "floater" — a special add-on to your policy. It's smart to videotape all your possessions (storing the tape outside the house). *If your house has smoke detectors and a security system, make sure you're getting at least a 2% premium discount.*

Alert! ***Like many other insurance plans, raising your deductible can really drop your premium.***

KEEP IN MIND! Be very cautious of "perpetual" policies that cover your home for as long as you own it for one huge, up-front premium. Here's why: You'd better stay in the house for a very long time (and hope the insurance company stays in business!). If your house goes up in value over time, you'll need to pay extra to boost coverage.

Alert! ***Renters should have coverage for their furniture and other belongings. That's the only way you can collect after a fire or theft; your landlord has no responsibility. Plus, it's a good idea to have liability coverage in these lawsuit-happy days.***

Liability Insurance protects you in case you're sued. Normally both your homeowner's and auto plans contain liability protection. Homeowner's covers you and all family members living in the house even if the accident didn't happen within the residence. (A neighbor slips and falls on your front walk, for example.) If you hurt someone or damage their property while driving, your car insurance offers protection.

L **ife Insurance** — There are 3 major types :

Term, the cheapest since it provides "pure" death protection. You die and your beneficiary gets the policy's face amount. You live and it has no value whatsoever. Term is purchased in short intervals with the price going up as your age increases. Should you develop a serious health problem, finding replacement coverage could be difficult, very expensive and maybe unobtainable. (While most term plans permit the policyholder to "convert" or switch over to a more permanent plan, the cost can also be stiff.) Regardless, term insurance is still the best way to get maximum protection for the least amount of dollars for a specific period of years. *Many companies offer special low rates (called preferred non-smoker) for healthy people who do not smoke.*

Whole Life, or "permanent" insurance, combines the death protection of term with a tax-deferred savings capability. You pay a fixed premium for life — or a specific number of years — that, unlike term, builds cash values (based on a set schedule) that can be withdrawn or borrowed. While more expensive than term, you don't have to worry about finding new coverage if your health becomes a factor. You can also add on various riders — policy additions such as spouse and children's coverage, waiver of premium (should you become disabled and unable to make the premium payment), etc. **Universal Life**, like Whole Life, emphasizes the investment/savings aspect of insurance but on a much more flexible basis. With Universal Life, your premium goes directly into a kind of cash-building account — out of which your cost for insurance protection is deducted monthly. The balance in your account is credited with a "current" interest rate which is designed to reflect contemporary interest rates. (There is also a "guaranteed" rate — kind of a safety net under which your plan can never drop.) Unlike whole life, you can make changes in your plan automatically — like raising or lowering your coverage, even skipping premium payments etc. Plus, you get an annual statement that details your cash values, amount of coverage, amounts borrowed or withdrawn, etc.

Alert! ***Beware of buying a Universal Life plan solely on the current interest rate credited to your policy. One plan may offer an 8% interest rate but deduct considerably more for the "death protection" portion than a company that pays 7 1/2% with a lower cost of coverage. Watch out for "cancer" and "dread disease" plans that are both costly and provide very fragmented protection at best.***

Joint policies (issued on both spouses or couples) offer a substantial savings — as much as 30% or more — versus the purchase of two individual policies.

Finally, there is another type of insurance called **Variable Life** that tries to provide *death benefits* — not cash values — that rise with inflation. Your policy goes up (or down) based on how well the investments tied to your plan perform. While there is a potential upside, the concept has more risk since benefits are unknown. *And remember, the reason you buy life insurance is guaranteed death protection.* Life insurance proceeds (paid to your beneficiary) are not subject to federal income taxes no matter what the type of plan. *They are, however, subject to federal and state estate taxes.*

Wash Loans allow you to tap into your cash values on a tax-free basis. Aggressively promoted by many life insurance companies, it works like this: you *borrow* the cash value (tax free) out of your policy rather than withdraw it. The interest you're charged on the loan exactly equals the interest earned in your policy. *It's a wash!* You never pay back the loan. (The unborrowed cash left in the policy keeps the policy in force.) At some point down the line, you may have to come up with some extra premium to keep the policy from lapsing.

Alert! ***If your policy lapses, you not only lose protection, but you could face all sorts of tax problems.***

Long-Term Nursing Home Care Insurance is designed to provide what other policies generally do not: extended care for those people not seriously ill but who need day-to-day help. (LTC is called "coverage for people worrying about living too long, rather than dying too soon.") Currently, it can cost anywhere from $35,000 to $60,000 a year to stay in a nursing home. If you have a modest income and are over age 60, check out your Medicaid eligibility and perhaps save the expense of a couple thousand dollars or more in annual premium. If you're of a moderate to high income, consider a policy that provides unlimited number of days with at least an $80 to $90 a day benefit *and has inflation protection.* Statistically speaking, your chances of entering and staying in a nursing home longer than a few years are quite small. Singles, living alone, probably have a greater need. (By definition, a **nursing home** offers around-the-clock medical care and supervision; a **personal care home** helps "residents" with their daily routines — eating, bathing, taking medication, etc.)

Alert! ***These plans are expensive. Any one you consider should cover "custodial" as well as medical care, be "guaranteed renewable" (which means it can't be cancelled as long as you pay your premium), and include Alzheimer's medical/disorder benefits. Read the fine print. "Type of care," waiting periods, deductibles, and "exclusions" can vary all over the place. Stick with an A+ company that won't go belly-up!***

Medicaid is a health insurance program for low-income people and families. Eligibility rules vary from state to state but Medicaid generally provides medical assistance to people already under cash assistance programs, or those deemed "medically needy" by the state.

Medicare is a federal health insurance program for virtually everyone over age 65. There are basically two parts: **Part A,** which covers hospital stays. (There is a $676 annual deductible.) And **Part B,** which covers various out-of-hospital expenses. (There is a $36.60 charge per month that's deducted from your social security check.) Although Part B is optional, you're automatically enrolled unless you elect not to take it. Other Medicare options include: **Home Health (Convalescent) Care** (in-home assistance relating to an accident or chronic illness); **Hospice**, which provides support services for dying patients and their families; and **Prescription Drugs**, which are reimbursable after a deductible is satisfied. (There is a co-payment — or "cost sharing" involved, with you paying around 40% of the tab.)

Supplemental Medicare Insurance, commonly called "Medigap Insurance," is designed to plug the gap or pick up those expenses not covered by Medicare. Recently, Medigap policies have been standardized, making it much easier for side-by-side comparisons of plans. Countless senior citizens have been duped into buying plans that are too costly and unnecessary. If you've just turned 65, you can't be denied coverage because of health problems during an "open-enrollment" six-month period.

Alert! ***Here are some Medigap buying tips: (1) Make sure the policy is guaranteed renewable — so you can't be cancelled; (2) Find out if the plan you're considering excludes "pre-existing" health conditions; (3) Consider an "excess-charges" benefit only if the doctors in your area charge more than the Medicare rate; (4) Do not drop one Medigap policy until you've been accepted under a new one; (5) Don't buy or switch plans exclusively on price (the insurer's financial strength and efficiency in paying claims is especially important); (6) Think about a plan that covers Medicare's 1993 deductible of $676 (which you could incur several times a year — it's not a one-time annual deductible); (7) Get independent advice through associations like the AARP (the American Association of Retired Persons).***

Title Insurance protects you from buying a house (or piece of property) a seller doesn't legally own — or which has a lien or easement against it. It comes in two forms: lender's coverage, which protects the mortgage company (on the money they lend you), and owner's coverage, which insures the total value of the property. You pay for both — although owner's is optional since it's for your protection. There is a one-time premium charge.

Umbrella Policies are added limits liability policies that offer coverage of $1 million or more over and above the basic homeowner limit. As the name suggests, these policies also provide broader protection for such things as libel or invasion of privacy suits. (Ask your insurance company about a quantity discount if you consolidate all your property/casualty coverages — auto, homeowners and umbrella.)

Terminology, Techniques & Taxes

- Asset Allocation
- Back-Up Withholding
- Bank Ratings Information
- Blue List
- Book Value
- Capital Gain/Home Exclusion
- Closing Costs
- Collection Agencies
- Complaints
- Credit Cards
- Credit Reports
- Credit Unions
- Discount Brokers
- Dividend Reinvestment Plans (DRIPS)
- Dollar Cost Averaging
- Dow Jones/S&P
- ERISA
- Escrow
- Estate Taxes
- Extended Warranty
- Federal Reserve
- Financial Planners
- Gifts
- Investment Clubs
- IPOs
- Liquidity
- Living Wills
- Managed Competition
- Options
- Power of Attorney
- Price/Earnings Ratio
- Prime Rate
- Property Taxes
- Prospectus
- Rating Services
- Refinancing/Mortgage Pay-Off
- Rollovers & Lump-Sum Withdrawals
- Rule of 72
- Selling Short
- Stock Exchanges
- Street Name/Stock Transfer
- Systematic Withdrawal Plans
- Taxes
- Trusts & Wills
- Workers Comp
- Wrap Accounts

Asset Allocation is a way to spread out your money in a variety of both growth and stable income accounts (say, some in stocks, some in bonds, some in a money market fund, etc.). How you split it up is based on a lot of factors, including your years until retirement, need for income, tolerance for risk, etc. Because you haven't put all your eggs in one basket you've diffused risk by covering all the bases no matter what happens in the marketplace. *A balanced mutual fund is designed to accomplish this mix.*

Back-Up Withholding will occur if you don't give the bank, mutual fund, or any other place you receive earnings your social security number. You do this by filling out a W-9 form with each payer of interest and dividends, etc.

Alert! ***Beginning in 1993, if you fail to give your social security number to the appropriate institutions, 31% of all earnings will be withheld and sent to the IRS.***

Bank Ratings Information can be found by calling Veribanc at 800 44-BANKS; Bauer Financial Reports at 800 388-6686; or Sheshunoff Information Services at 800 456-2340.
Recent federal regulations have new solvency standards. It will cost you $10 or so to get your bank ratings by one of these services. First, make sure your bank is insured by the Federal Deposit Insurance Corp. (FDIC). *Second, make sure that all accounts in any one bank (or savings & loan) don't exceed $100,000 — that means the total of all checking, savings plans, CDs, etc., including accrued interest! However, you can set up your accounts so ownership is spread around to create separate deposits — with each getting the FDIC coverage.* (By the way, a bank's "nonperforming assets" are just another way of saying their "bad loans.")

Blue List is a daily price quotation for tax-free municipals (published by Standard & Poor's) used by most brokerage firms and banks.

Book Value represents the net worth of a company. Commonly referred to as the liquidating value (what the company is worth should it go out of business), book value is determined by subtracting what the company owes from what it owns. If you divide that figure by the total number of outstanding shares, you'll get the per-share book value. If that number is more than the current stock price, the company is selling under book and represents a buy signal to many investors.

Capital Gain Exclusion (from federal income tax) on the sale of your principal residence is available to anyone 55 or older. You do not have to pay capital gains tax on up to $125,000 of the profit, providing you have owned and lived there three of the five years before the sale. You can only exercise this exclusion 1 time! Normally, if you sell your house, you have 24 months to buy another one at an equal or greater price to avoid paying capital gains tax. Currently, capital gains are taxed at 15% if you're in the 15% federal tax bracket and 28% if you're in either the 28% or 31% bracket. You can reduce any gain by the cost of all additions and improvements you've made to the house — but not simple maintenance and repairs.

Closing Costs on the purchase of a home include the points (an up-front interest charge — see below) the lender adds to your loan; the cost of title insurance (which protects the lender if the title is not free and clear); the lender's attorney fees; fees for termite inspection; a survey of the property; and often, an escrow account **(see separate heading)** to pay property taxes and homeowners insurance. *(Each point equals 1% of the amount borrowed. A $100,000 mortgage with 2 points costs you $2,000.)* You probably also will be charged with a mortgage application fee, an appraisal fee, a credit report fee and various other filing and notary costs. Federal regulations demand that the lender supply you a good-faith estimate of these settlement costs within 3 days after you apply for the loan. *Consider an Adjustable Rate Mortgage (ARM) only if you plan to stay a relatively short time in the home — around 3 years or so. With an ARM, your interest rate can be adjusted every year, or 3 years, etc. (depending on the type) within limits or caps.*

Alert! ***Some lenders promote "no point' mortgages but fail to tell you about the loan origination fee. It's nothing more than a finance charge that also runs around 1% of the amount borrowed. Points, by the way, are profit for the lender and may be negotiable.***

Collection Agencies can be abusive and unrelenting. Federal law states debt collectors can't harass you at "unreasonable times or places." (8:00 A.M.–9:00 P.M. are considered reasonable hours.) If any strong-arm tactics are used against you, keep track of the times and dates. The collection agency is required to send you — *within 5 days of the first contact* — written notice of what is owed and the procedure you should follow if the debt is incorrect.

Alert! ***To protect yourself, you must answer the notice by certified mail within 30 days, either disputing the amount owed or stating you are aware of the debt. This letter stops the collection agency in its tracks, preventing any further abuse.***

Complaints in an investment dispute (with a stockbroker) can be directed in writing to either New York Stock Exchange, Arbitration Department, 20 Broad Street-5th Floor, New York, NY 10005 (212-656-2772); American Stock Exchange, Investor Inquiries, 86 Trinity Place, New York, NY 10006 (212-306-1452); National Association of Securities Dealers (contact your local district office or write to Surveillance Dept., 1735 K Street, N.W., Washington, DC 20006). The NASD also has a hot line (800-289-9999) that discloses any disciplinary actions taken against member brokers. You may also contact your state securities regulator. At the government level, address the Securities & Exchange Commission, Office of Consumer Affairs, 450

5th Street N.W., Room 2115, Washington, DC 20549 (202-272-7440). If you've got an insurance problem get in touch with your State Insurance Department.

Credit Card spending has been the "Svengalli" of financial stress for countless people. Ask yourself: Do you know — off the top of your head — how much you owe? (Is it 10%, 15% or more of your disposable income?) If you finance a purchase with your card over 6 months or so, you should factor in the interest you'll pay to the price of the item. (The savings you achieve by buying something on sale can be more than offset by the financing costs.)

KEEP IN MIND! The "average" consumer pays around $400 to $500 a year in interest charges that are *not* tax deductible! Don't keep a lot of credit cards you don't use. The more you have, the more nervous lenders get, because of the tab you can run up on each one.

A **Secured Credit Card** is an option for people who have been turned down or have no credit history. Basically, the lender requires you to set up a CD or savings account (as a kind of collateral) with *that* amount becoming your charge limit. A **Debit Card** draws out money from an already established checking or savings account (somewhat like an ATM card). Since your account is "debited" automatically each time you use the card, there is *no grace period* — eliminating your ability to hold up payment if there is a dispute of some kind. While there are no bigger-than-expected "surprises" at the end of the month, you could "overdraft" your account without knowing it. Finally, some banks have various "user" fees!

Alert! ***When choosing a credit card, consider not only the interest rate, which can vary all over the lot, but also the length of the grace period, membership fees, transaction and late charges, etc. Check with Bankcard Holders of America for the scoop on virtually any credit card. Also, there's a new merchandising gimmick called "save as you spend." In a nutshell, the credit card company will contribute a part (about 5% or 6%) of the total amount you charge into a "savings account" for you. The problem is you have to "spend to save " — and you must buy only from participating merchants!***

Credit Reports can be obtained from the following leading bureaus: Equifax, P. O. Box 4091, Atlanta, GA 30302; TRW / P. O. Box 5450, Orange, CA 92667; Trans. Union, 444 N. Michigan Ave., Chicago IL 60611. (TRW will give you the first one at no charge, while the others charge a few dollars.) If you are ever refused credit, you are entitled to a copy of your report for free. By the way, black marks for bankruptcy stay on your record for 7–10 years.

Alert! ***Check up on your report every year or so. With mistakes and inaccuracies rampant, it's a good idea to order a copy and examine it before some problem unexpectedly pops up!***

Credit Unions are really nonprofit cooperatives that operate like banks for their members. Since they are operated solely for the benefit of their members and operate without a lot of overhead, credit unions generally provide very attractive savings and loan rates. Credit Unions are quite safe, with the great majority covered by the National Credit Union Share Insurance Fund (NCUSIF), a federal agency that insures deposits like the FDIC does for banks.

Discount Brokers allow you to buy or sell securities at a reduced trading fee. You do not get the advice or recommendations you would from a full-service brokerage house.

Dividend Reinvestment Plans (DRIPS) allow shareholders to buy more stock with their dividends — and to make additional cash purchases — on a little or no fee/commission basis. (If the dividend is not large enough to buy one full share, you are given "fractional" shares.) DRIPS are most appropriate for long-term investors who want to plough back all their earnings into additional shares. Mutual funds, in most cases, automatically reinvest earnings unless you instruct them otherwise.

Dollar Cost Averaging is an investment technique where you invest a set amount of dollars on a set schedule without interruption. For example, suppose you invest $100 a month in mutual fund X on a regular basis. In month #l, assume the fund's share price is $10 — giving you 10 shares. The next month the fund's price goes up to $12 a share — giving you 8⅓ shares. The following month the fund's price drops to $8 a share — giving you 12½ shares for the same $100 investment. And so on. Over time, you will have purchased more shares when the price is low and fewer shares when the price is high — eliminating the guess work of market timing. *Mathematically, you'll come out ahead since you bought more shares below the average value and less above the average value.* You can't "cry uncle," however! To make this averaging technique work, you have to maintain your investment schedule *continuously* during both bull and bear markets.

KEEP IN MIND! If you plan on making a large, single investment, it's smart to park that cash in a money market account — having a portion automatically transferred to the mutual fund (or investment) of your choice every month or quarter. This way you avoid the risk of bad market timing — the chance you'll invest everything when share prices are high!

Dow Jones Industrial Average tracks the performance of 30 select industrial blue chip stocks. The Dow is considered the *leading indicator* because the companies were chosen from sectors of the economy most representative of our nation's industrial vitality. **The Standard & Poors S&P 500** is a *broader* market index since it follows 500 companies. The Wilshire 5,000 goes further by keeping an eye on 5,000 companies. (All these indexes are called "unmanaged" since they simply track results.) What you hear on TV and the radio at the end of each business day is how those 30 "Dow" stocks did — not what the whole market did. (When the announcer says, "The market was up 11 points today," he or she is really talking about the average gain of just those 30 companies.)

ERISA ("Employee Retirement Income Security Act") is a federal law that regulates pension plans and other employee benefits, including health insurance. *Basically, it protects both the security of the pension funds and the rights of each participant to make sure he or she gets what's promised.*

E **scrow** is an account set up between you and the home mortgage lender at closing. It's a forced method of collecting the estimated cost of your property taxes and hazard insurance (and private mortgage insurance, if any) and is *required* by most lenders. This estimated cost is broken down into 12 monthly payments and *added* on to your mortgage payment. (The term PITI is used to describe escrow — principal, interest, taxes, insurance.) The only upside to escrow is that when your tax and insurance bills come due, the money is already there. The downside is the lender gets to use your money over the year without giving you any interest. Plus, it's up to your lender to promptly pay those bills — or you get the late notices!

Alert! ***Overcharges can be the rule rather than the exception — particularly with adjustable rate mortgages. Moreover, if you were required to buy private mortgage insurance (PMI), that cost should stop once you have 20% equity in your home.***

E **state Taxes** — which start at 18% and can reach 55% — are incurred on anything you leave your heirs over $600,000. (There is a rumored move to slash the limit to $200,000.) However, there is no limit (or current tax liability) on assets left to a spouse — called an unlimited marital deduction. When the second spouse dies, however, the entire value of the estate is then taxable, potentially leaving the heirs with a big tax headache. (A "*Second-to Die*" life insurance policy, which pays off when the second spouse dies, can help satisfy the tax for those with larger estates. An *irrevocable life insurance trust* accomplishes about the same thing — and allows the second spouse to draw income until he or she passes.) **See Trusts & Wills.** *Remember, life insurance proceeds are exempt from income tax but not from the inheritance tax.*

Alert! ***All states (except Nevada) have their own estate or inheritance tax in addition to the federal tax bite — and they come into play at much lower amounts. Planning is critical to avoid the erosion of your accumulated assets.***

Extended **Warranties** are generally not a good idea. Sold to provide extended coverage beyond the basic warranty for such items as cars, they are usually not necessary and are quite costly.

Alert! ***There have been a lot of consumer complaints with these warranties, particularly when purchased from an independent company rather than your dealer. Regardless, expect a lot of high pressure because they are very profitable — particularly for the sales person, who makes a big up-front commission.***

Federal **Reserve** sets interest rates that are charged to member banks in the federal system. As the country's central bank, it directly affects your borrowing costs. A *cut* in rates frees up capital (or the money supply) to member banks, theoretically stimulating growth. An *increase* in rates restricts borrowing, theoretically cooling the economy and the threat of inflation. The "Fed" also influences interest rates by setting the reserve requirements — funds the bank must set aside to protect depositors.

Financial Planners can be a stock broker, an insurance agent, an accountant, virtually any of a variety of unregulated advisors. (Certified Financial Planners [CFP] have passed certain educational requirements.) They get paid in two ways: **(1)** You pay a fee based on the size of your account and the performance achieved, or for the time spent consulting with you, or **(2)** You get charged a commission based on the products sold you.

Alert! ***Be very careful of anyone working on a commission basis. These planners may be predisposed - even limited - by only the products they are authorized to sell. While good advice is always worth the price, weigh your need for such services as well as the cost.***

By definition, a financial planner looks at your whole financial picture creating an overall strategy or plan. A stock broker advises and trades securities. A money manager manages assets you've already accumulated.

Gifts can be made by an individual to a child — or anyone else — up to $10,000 a year without incurring any gift tax. (The limit is $20,000 if jointly given by both spouses.) This limit affects only the giver. The recipient has no such restriction. Gifts can be many things, such as securities, real estate, collectibles, etc., as well as cash. Noncash gifts are based on the present value of the gift on the date it is given. *There is no gift tax to the recipient and no federal forms to fill out. You can give a gift (under the "gift-to-minors act" or the more recent "transfer to minors act"), naming yourself as custodian. You'll maintain control even though the child owns the gift, including all future earnings and taxes due.* Beginning in 1993, a child up to age 14 can receive up to $1,200 per year in interest or dividends before he or she is taxed at the parent's rate. Many well-off seniors make gifts to reduce their net worth to $600,000 (or lower) to avoid any inheritance tax on what they leave behind.

Investment Clubs are everyday people who pool their money to buy stocks selected by (and agreed upon) by the whole group. They generally stick to the "basics" — buy and hold stocks with growth rates of at least 15% a year. Sometimes, they invite professionals to speak to their group, advise them on their picks, and execute their trades. All members share in the profit or bear the loss on a proportional basis.

IPOs are Initial Public Offerings that occur when a privately owned company goes public — that means they sell stock to you or me to raise capital. (In the process, management sweat is turned into instant riches since they're selling investors part of their company.) After this *initial* offering, shares then trade on the *secondary* market — that is, the major stock exchanges. Recent changes in the law have both expedited and simplified the IPO process. Interest in small company shares are soaring with IPOs riding the popular wave.

Alert! ***While IPOs offer a ground-floor opportunity in high potential companies, investors should approach with caution. You need to know the industry involved, the company's track record (many are "fledgling" businesses), its rate of return, among other things. IPOs can be volatile and puffed up by a lot of hype.***

Liquidity is simply the ability to sell an asset quickly. (The classic definition includes *without a loss.*) Cashing in a money market account has a high level of liquidity. Mutual funds can be sold in minutes, but there's no guarantee you'll get all your money back at the time you sell. Real Estate or long-term annuities are more frozen assets if you want to unload them quickly.

Living Wills are documents that specify whether you wish to continue on life support if and when your medical condition is terminal. This prevents the family from having to make the painful decision of when "to pull the plug." A living will can be written simply and without a lawyer. It should be witnessed by at least two adults and notarized.

Managed Competition is a health insurance reform proposal that's receiving a lot of attention by some high-level movers and shakers. Basically, the concept permits employers and individuals to buy health insurance through a giant, nonprofit cooperative. (The government would pick up the tab for the poor and unemployed.) The co-op would negotiate with networks of hospitals, doctors and insurance companies, who would compete among themselves for the contracts. All of these medical networks would have to offer a standardized benefit package from which consumers could choose. No one can be denied coverage and everyone would pay about the same amount. The raging debate rests with the cost this concept will have on small business, who may be required to either pay for their workers' insurance outright or pay a premium into a public fund to cover them.

Options are essentially orders to buy or sell securities at a certain price at a certain time. There are two types: a call option is the buy order, and a put option is the sell order. Options let you play your hunches about which way a stock could go without buying the stock at full value. (Options are called *derivatives* because they "derive" their value from some underlying investment.) Options cost a fraction of the share price. The newspapers list their prices daily. If things don't go the way you thought, you can let the option run out — and you're out only the cost of the option. *Here's a very simplified example. Suppose you think company X stock is going to take off from its current level of $50. You buy a call option for $5, which gives you the right to buy company X stock up to some future date at the current $50 price. Let's say your hunch pays off and the stock zooms to $70 a share. You exercise your option to buy at the $50 price and make a net $15 per share profit. On the other hand, let's say you're wrong, and the company drops or goes nowhere. You simply let the option expire and you're out only the $5.* Basically, options limit the potential for big losses while leaving open the door for big gains. As you can see, it's a technique investors use to hedge their bets. **Company stock options** are employee perks that give you the right to buy company stock at a set price. If that stock goes up in the future, you can exercise your option and buy the stock at the lower option price.

KEEP IN MIND! Four times a year, you'll hear the term "triple witching hour." That's the time when both options and futures expire simultaneously. It occurs on the third Friday of the last month of each quarter and generally triggers a lot of wild trading activity. **(See Selling Short Section.)**

Power of Attorney gives some other party (a spouse, trusted friend or adult child) the right to sign checks and conduct other business on your behalf. This power can be revoked at any time.

Price/Earnings Ratio is the price of the stock divided by the earnings per share. It is an indicator of how the stock is priced. *All you need to remember is the higher the number the more overpriced or speculative the stock has become.*

Prime Rate is considered the best rate available from the bank. It is reserved for the bank's best customers and serves as a yardstick for the level of interest rates charged to the rest of us.

P**roperty Taxes** can be challenged at your tax assessor's office. You should first request your "property record card" to make sure all the specs on your house are accurate. (The square footage is right, the lot size is correct, etc.) You will also need comparable sale information (what houses similar to yours recently sold for) to make your case.

P**rospectus** is a required document mutual funds and other stock-based plans (and "new offerings," etc.) have to give you before you invest. Without exception, they are difficult to read — and more difficult to understand. The type of information they offer include: investment goals and policies; the type and allocation of investments; the risk involved; the management team; total performance; various fees and charges; etc. There is a move underway to simplify the prospectus.

R**ating Services** include the following: for bonds, Moody, Standard & Poors; insurance, A.M. Best, Duff & Phelps, Moody's, Standard & Poors, Weiss Research; mutual funds, Lipper, Morningstar, etc.

R**efinancing** your home should be considered only if you lower your interest rate by at least 2% points and you plan to stay put for 5 years or more. Get a 15-year mortgage if you can afford the monthly payment — you'll save a bundle in interest over the years. It makes sense to pay off your mortgage early (if you're able to), *unless you can earn a return significantly higher than your home loan interest rate. Today, that's pretty tough to do, particularly when you factor in the tax deductible "savings" of your mortgage interest.* (For example, if you had a 9% mortgage, you would have to get around 11% or so elsewhere just to break even.) Paying down your mortgage by sending in extra principal payments on a regular basis is always a good idea.

Rollover is simply the ability to personally move retirement-oriented funds to a different account *without* incurring taxes. (For instance, if you want to switch your IRA account from a bank to a mutual fund, you've got 60 days — from withdrawal to redeposit — to do it.) Lump-sum withdrawals, however, from any kind of company retirement plan (including pensions, 401k's, etc.) face a potential new tax trap! No longer can you make a simple tax-free rollover yourself without getting hit with a double whammy: (1) 20% of your funds will be withheld, and (2) that 20% will be considered taxable income. *To avoid the tax and any penalty, you'll have to "replace" that 20% from your own pocket — which you'll get back as an income tax refund.* (Also if you take that money out before you're old enough — because you change jobs, get laid off or retire early — you'll get slapped with an additional penalty.)

Alert! ***To escape all these hassles, let your "old" retirement plan pay the funds directly to your new one. This is called a trustee-to-trustee transfer.* The key is not to take possession *of your nest egg!***

KEEP IN MIND! Forward averaging is a method of computing tax on a lump-sum retirement settlement. While the tax is still due all at once, it has the net effect of reducing your tax rate. (For example, a $100,000 cash withdrawal is computed as though you were receiving $10,000 a year for 10 years.)

Rule of 72 is a simple formula to determine how long it takes to double your money. Just divide the current rate of return into 72. For example, if you're getting 9% interest on a CD, it will take you 8 years to double your money. (72 ÷ 9% = 8 years.) A 6% interest rate would take 12 years (72÷ 6% = 12 years).

Selling Short is selling a stock you don't have. You borrow shares from a brokerage house because you have a hunch the price is going down. If you're right, you can buy "replacement" shares at the lower price repaying the broker, pocketing the difference. If you're wrong and the stock goes up, you're obligated to pay back the broker with higher-priced shares with no limit on how much you can lose.

Alert! ***Selling short — particularly for the average investor — is like playing with dynamite! Do not go near this high-risk trading maneuver or others like buying and selling futures (which can be stocks, commodities, precious metals, etc.). Buying stock on margin is another very dangerous technique where you borrow up to half the price of the stock from your broker (generally at an interest rate slightly above prime).***

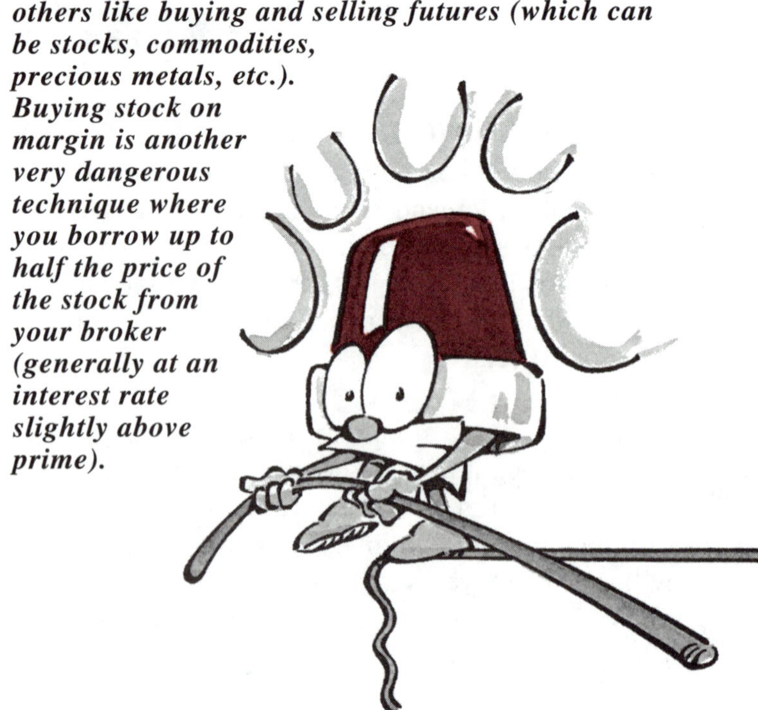

Stock Exchanges are the arenas — the "marketplace" — where company shares are continually bought and sold. (Without them, you would have to find a buyer or seller on your own.) There are three major ones: the New York (called the Big Board), the American (AMEX), and the NASDAQ (commonly called over-the-counter). There is a relationship between a company's size and what exchange it is listed. The giant, well-established blue-chips (like the 30 Dow Jones stocks) are usually listed on the New York, while the smaller, more speculative, start-up companies make up the NASDAQ. While the small cap NASDAQ companies are not tested by time, their lure is very strong since their potential is greater - as is their risk. (Investors try to catch a rising star on its way up.) Traditionally, the more successful a company becomes, the more likely it will move to the Big Board. Each of the major exchanges tracks the performance of its own stocks, publishing the results daily. **(See Dow Jones/S&P Section.)** *What happens if the whole market panics — plunging stocks into a tailspin? All trading simply shuts down. It's called a "Circuit Breaker," and it gives jittery investors a chance to cool off.*

Street Name is how stocks — purchased by you but held by your brokerage house — are referred to. Although the broker is technically the registered owner, you are the real (or beneficial) owner. Many investors like the broker to hold their stock (rather than take possession of the actual certificates) for safety and ease in trading.

Alert! ***Should you take possession of the actual certificates and lose them, you'll have to provide a lost-security affidavit and post a surety bond. This little ordeal will also cost you as much as 4% of the lost shares' market value.***

Changing stock ownership (through a gift or inheritance, etc.) starts with the **Transfer Agent.** You'll find the name and address in the shareholder report.

Systematic Withdrawal Plans, which are offered by many mutual funds, allow you to draw out a fixed dollar amount (or percentage) from your account on an automatic basis, usually monthly. Once dividends and capital gains are exhausted, shares are cashed in, dropping your account value. If you want to keep your account intact, have the fund send you just the earnings. *Be aware that some funds (called government-plus) have been accused of fattening up their shareholder returns by paying out principal along with the interest earned.*

Taxes. Currently, there are 3 tax brackets: 15%, 28% & 31%. The top one is applied to taxable incomes over $51,500 individually and $86,500 for married couples filing jointly. To avoid penalties associated with the underpayment of taxes (called a safe harbor), at least 90% of the tax you owe must have been withheld by January 15. The self-employed must do this through quarterly estimated tax payments. *(The top tax rate could rise to 36% — with an added "surcharge" on $250,000 incomes — if some current proposals being tossed around become law.)* In 1993, personal exemptions have been increased to $2,300 while the standard deduction has been raised to $6,000 on joint returns, $3,600 on single returns, and $5,250 for heads of households.

KEEP IN MIND! The Alternative Minimum Tax (AMT) is a kind of equalization tax that usually affects the wealthy who use various deductions and preferences to reduce (or eliminate) their tax liability. The intent of the AMT is to collect a fair share from these people by requiring them to use a difference method of calculating their tax.

Alert! ***Taxpayers Have a Bill of Rights!***

If you get an audit notice (or a demand by mail for a tax adjustment), don't become unglued. The computer may have red-flagged your return through the IRS's electronic screening process and not because you made a mistake. (Unless, of course, you have "fudged" your return and you tripped one of the major triggers.) The first and most important thing to do is dig up all your records that support your income and deductions. Try to get the dispute resolved through the mail rather than a face-to-face interview. If you can't — and the date the IRS wants you to come in is a problem — request a mutually convenient time. Remember, an auditor has no power to force you to change your return without your consent. Plus, you have the right to challenge any penalties involved. If you don't get satisfaction, you can go to the examiner's supervisor, air your grievances through the problem resolution process or the IRS's Appeals Office, and ultimately take your case to the U.S. Tax Court. (You may face a lot of time-consuming paperwork along the way.) If you agree you do owe back taxes but are unable to pay in full, negotiate an installment schedule.

Alert! ***Don't blindly accept what the IRS says carte blanche just to keep them off your back. They've been wrong too many times. Keep good records and be prepared to make your case.***

Here's just a few tax-planning ideas worth considering:

- Pay real estate and state income taxes before year end — and you can write off the entire amount in the current year. (This reduces your taxable income.)
- Sell stock that has gone down in value and *deduct* up to $3,000 (of that "capital" loss) from your salary or other income. You can write off a capital loss against a capital gain dollar for dollar. You can't sell a stock — take the loss — and buy it back again without waiting 30 days. (That's called a wash sale.)
- Make a charitable contribution of stock and you get a double tax benefit:
  (1) You get to deduct the full market value of the securities, and
  (2) You do not have to pay any capital gains tax on the profit built up over the years.
- Use your credit cards (near the end of the year) to make medical payments, charitable contributions, etc., and deduct the payment in

the year you charged it — even though you may not get the bill until next year. *(This is another way to lower your taxable income by maximizing deductions.)*

- Give a child (over age 14), who is probably in the lowest tax bracket, a stock that has really appreciated over the years. When the child sells the stock, that hefty capital gain will be taxed at his or her rate — not yours. Keep the stock gift under $10,000. **(See Gifts Section.)**
- Don't invest IRA contributions in securities (like municipal bond funds, annuities, etc.) that *already* are tax deferred! You're wasting part of your tax benefit!

If you are self-employed:

- You can deduct 28 cents per mile on your personal car used for business.
- If you have an office in your home, you can write off those expenses devoted exclusively for your business (on a proportionate basis). You can't have an office elsewhere to get this benefit.

KEEP IN MIND! The "Nanny" (social security tax) has to be withheld for any domestic help paid more than $50 per quarter. That means you have to apply for a federal employer I.D. number and make the appropriate filings and payments every quarter. You are not required to withhold income tax unless requested by the "nanny." If pay for household services reaches

$1,000 a quarter, state and federal unemployment taxes also come into play. Be sure to fill out U.S. Immigration and Naturalization Service Form I-9, required of all employees eligible to work in this country. Keep the form handy should a government inspector ever request it.

Trusts & Wills are instruments that allow you to pass your assets on to your heirs and to control the way they are used. If you die without a will (called intestate), your assets will be distributed by state law — not according to your wishes. Additionally, the probate court will appoint an administrator to carry out these duties rather than you having selected your own executor to follow through on your wishes. (Probate is the court process in which your property is inventoried, accounted for and dispersed.)

Alert! ***The key here is to avoid the cost and delays of probate by arranging your affairs so that you have very little in your own name at the time of death. You can do this through joint ownership of your assets with rights of survivorship. Your assets are owned jointly by you and someone you designate where — upon the death of either — all assets pass to the survivor automatically and without probate.***

When you set up and transfer assets to a trust, you relinquish legal ownership of them (although you can name yourself trustee and control the assets any way you like). By doing this, those assets are not legally owned by you and avoid the probate process as well. It is said that trusts "don't take life from your death." They permit you to maintain personal control and have your instructions faithfully followed while you're alive or disabled. (A trust also offers greater assurance that your wishes be followed beyond putting your property in joint tenancy.) There are various kinds of trusts, from "living" to "irrevocable." Unlike a will, a living trust does not have to go through probate. *(Life insurance proceeds also escape probate and go directly to your heirs. They do not, however, escape estate taxes.)*

Alert! ***Avoid buying do-it-yourself trust kits which generally are rip-offs marketed by high-pressure sales organizations. Also, don't confuse a living trust with a living will. The latter expresses your wishes regarding the continuation of life support in terminal health situations.***

Workers Compensation paid by your employer covers you if you are injured on the job, whether it's your fault or not. You can't sue your employer unless there is some gross negligence involved, but you do receive a guarantee that medical, rehabilitation and job-retraining costs (plus a percentage of lost wages) be paid for you.

Wrap Accounts are all-in-one accounts (generally available through a brokerage house) for people with a lot of money. For one all-inclusive annual fee (up to 3% of your account value), your money is turned over to a professional manager who creates a portfolio of stocks and bonds and does all the trading. (Money management and brokerage commissions are wrapped into one flat charge.) Theoretically, these outside resources have superior experience and knowledge in money matters since they also manage the affairs of large corporate, pension and trustee accounts. In other words, as an individual investor you get access to their big-time expertise. Like all investments, performance, cost and independence of the money manager has to be evaluated.

LOST IN FINANCIAL AMERICA CAN HELP YOU FIND YOUR WAY.

As we enter a time of unparalleled change, the need to understand the basic financial forces that govern our present and future prosperity has never been greater. Now there is an easy-to-use tool to help you begin hammering away at that big mental block we've all built up!

Lost in Financial America can boost your knowledge and confidence level quicker than you ever thought possible! The book you wished someone would write has finally been written.

Sy Gitelson is president and owner of Atlanta-based Gitel & Associates, a national creative marketing/promotional firm that specializes in insurance, investment products and financial services.

Robbie Short is an illustrator/designer located in Atlanta, Georgia.